Hide-and-Seek Mon

Peek inside the closet.
Look underneath the bed.
You may get a glimpse
of a tail or a head.

**Don't forget the attic.
Monsters like to hide up there.**

4

Look behind the curtains.
Look beneath the stairs.

5

If you're scared of monsters,

here's one thing you can do.

Tiptoe up behind one

and softly whisper, "Boo!"

7

Search along the highway.
Search underneath the bridge.

Monsters like to stuff themselves,
so check inside the fridge.

9

When you are washing dishes,
look underneath the sink.
You might see an ogre
or meet the missing link.

if you're scared of monsters,

here's one thing you can do.

Tiptoe up behind one

and softly whisper, "Boo!"

Look inside the trash can.
Are there feet sticking out?

Peek into the pantry.
Can you see a monster snout?

14

Check behind the sofa.
Shine a flashlight underneath.
You may see big monster eyes.
You may see monster teeth.

Don't be scared of monsters
no matter what you do.

Remember that the monsters
are just as scared of **you!**